AKHIL KUMAR

"Mindfulness guide for beginners: The sattvic path to Wellness "

"Unleash the Transformative Power of Mindful practices and yogic diet for Health and Weight Loss in Just few pages of Enlightening Wisdom"

First edition

This book was professionally typeset on Reedsy.
Find out more at reedsy.com

This book is dedicated to all those whose lives have touched mine, igniting a fire within me to make a difference. To the patients I have had the privilege of caring for, their stories forever etched in my heart,

To those who are suffering mentally and emotionally, may these pages offer solace and guidance, illuminating a path toward healing and inner peace. Your strength and resilience inspire me every day. May this book serve as a beacon of hope, illuminating the path of towards wellness.

"To the wounded hearts and weary souls, May these words embrace and console. In every line, a whispered embrace, For those who've known life's toughest chase.

To the broken spirits and troubled minds, May this book offer solace, you shall find. In its pages, a gentle guiding light, To guide you through the darkest of nights.

For every tear shed and burden carried, Know that you're seen, your pain is not buried. In this dedication, a heartfelt vow, To honor your journey, then and now."

Contents

1

Introduction

Introduction

Welcome to a transformative journey that will change the way you think about food and wellness. This is not just another diet book. This is a guide to a new way of living, a path that intertwines the ancient wisdom of Sattvic eating with the powerful practice of mindfulness.

Join me, a doctor, seasoned dietician and mindfulness practitioner, as we delve into the philosophy, science, and practical applications of these transformative practices. Together, we will explore the profound connection between what we eat, how we eat and how we live, and uncover the secrets to long-term health and wellness.

Imagine transforming your health in few pages. Imagine discovering a way of eating that not only nourishes your body but also calms your mind and uplifts your spirit. That's the power of Sattvic eating and mindfulness.

In this guide, you will find a wealth of knowledge, from the principles of Sattvic eating to the science behind mindfulness. You will discover healing recipes that promote weight loss and well-being, and learn how to bring mindfulness into your everyday life. Along the way, I will share personal anecdotes, scientific insights, and practical tips to guide you on your journey.

So, are you ready to embark on this journey of transformation? Are you ready to explore the science behind these practices, discover their benefits, and learn how they can help conquer chronic illnesses? If so, let's begin this journey together.

Fact: Studies have shown that mindfulness practices can reduce stress and anxiety, improve attention and memory, and promote self-regulation and empathy.

2

Understanding Sattvic Eating

Sattvic eating is a concept rooted in Ayurveda, an ancient system of medicine that originated in India. The term 'Sattvic' is derived from 'Sattva', a Sanskrit word that signifies purity, truth, and serenity. Sattvic foods, therefore, are those that are pure, clean, and abundant in prana - the universal life force.

The Sattvic diet is predominantly plant-based, consisting of fresh, seasonal, and locally sourced fruits, vegetables, grains, and legumes. It avoids foods that are overly processed, fermented, or aged. The diet also emphasizes the importance of how the food is prepared and consumed, promoting the practice of cooking and eating with mindfulness and gratitude.

But why should we consider adopting a Sattvic diet? The benefits are manifold. Sattvic foods are typically high in dietary fiber, antioxidants, and essential nutrients, promoting optimal health and preventing disease. They are also light and easy to digest, leading to a sense of physical lightness and mental clarity.

In the following chapters, we will delve deeper into these benefits, explore the connection between Sattvic eating and mindfulness, and discover how this diet can aid in weight loss and wellness. But for now, let's take a moment to appreciate the simplicity and wisdom of the Sattvic diet - a testament to the adage that we truly are what we eat.

Fact: Research has shown that plant-based diets, like the Sattvic diet, can lower the risk of chronic illnesses such as heart disease and diabetes.

3

The Science of Mindfulness

Mindfulness is a practice that has its roots in ancient Buddhist meditation, but its benefits are backed by modern science. It involves bringing one's attention to the present moment with curiosity and non-judgmental awareness.This simple act of being present has been shown to have profound effects on our mental and physical health.

Mindfulness can help reduce stress, improve focus, and increase emotional resilience. It can also help us develop a healthier relationship with food, which is where it ties in beautifully with the Sattvic diet.

In the next chapter, we will explore the connection between Sattvic eating and mindfulness, and how these two practices can complement each other. But for now, let's take a moment to appreciate the power of mindfulness - a tool that is always at our disposal, requiring nothing but our presence.

Fact: Research has shown that regular mindfulness practice can actually change the structure of your brain. It can increase the density of the prefrontal cortex, the part of the brain responsible for executive functions like decision-making and attention.

4

The Connection Between Sattvic Eating and Mindfulness

The principles of Sattvic eating and mindfulness are deeply interconnected, creating a synergy that can transform our relationship with food and our bodies. Both practices emphasize the importance of being present and conscious, turning ordinary actions into moments of profound awareness and appreciation.

When we bring mindfulness to the act of eating, it becomes more than just consumption. It becomes an opportunity to savor each bite, to truly taste the food, and to listen to our body's signals of hunger and fullness. This mindful approach to eating aligns perfectly with the Sattvic diet, which promotes conscious consumption of pure, clean, and nutritious foods.

When we eat mindfully, we are more likely to choose Sattvic foods that nourish our bodies and minds. We are also less likely to overeat or choose unhealthy foods, as we are fully aware of what we are consuming and how it makes us feel. This synergy between Sattvic eating and mindfulness can be a powerful tool for weight loss and wellness.

In the next chapter, we will delve into the world of healing recipes that embody the principles of Sattvic eating and mindfulness. We'll provide practical guidance on how to incorporate these practices into your daily life, transforming your meals into moments of mindful nourishment.

Fact: Mindful eating has been shown to improve dietary choices, reduce overeating, and promote a healthier relationship with food.

5

Healing Recipes for Weight Loss and Wellness

Embarking on a journey of Sattvic eating and mindfulness doesn't mean you have to compromise on flavor or satisfaction. In fact, it's quite the opposite. This chapter is your gateway to a world of culinary delights that not only tantalize your taste buds but also nourish your body and mind.

We'll explore a variety of healing recipes, each embodying the principles of Sattvic eating and mindfulness. From vibrant breakfasts to nourishing lunches, comforting dinners, these recipes are designed to fuel your body, nourish every cell, satisfy your palate and bring joy to your kitchen.

Sattvic Recipes and diet plan practical guide:

1. Instead of a detailed and concrete plan which people are not able to follow, the author has given a moldable plan with easy recipes(includes easy and wide range of delicious Sattvic recipes).

Why moldable? Anyone can use it and can change it accordingly(Add other things which are under the calorie limit of the diet plan without affecting the purpose)because the fundamental diet is fixed which covers the 80% of your daily requirement and the rest 20% you can change(a range of interesting recipes have been provided).

2.Though it differs depending on age and activity level, adult males generally require 2,000-3000 calories per day to maintain weight while adult females need around 1,600-2,400 according to the U.S Department of Health.

3.Fix the calorie requirement to 1600/day and follow the diet for some days and then experience what your body and mind is experiencing and accordingly you can add and subtract a little bit of calories.

4.This book aims at conscious and mindful eating so instead of making a concrete boring plan, the aim is to make you conscious about what and how much you should eat.Without touching fundamental diet you can play around as long as you are following these guidelines.(with this conscious eating author has done bodybuilding, cross-fit, played fighting sports like taekwondo and yoga).losing weight is just a byproduct of this process, author is more concerned about blossoming of consciousness.

5.Check your weight loss every week which should be around 1 pound/week.(Not more than that) and then adjust accordingly without hampering the fundamental diet.

6.Fundamental diet is structured in a way that it consists of all the necessary nutrients so that with losing weight you will not experience nutritional deficiency.

7.It's not in the scope of this book to mention all recipes including diet plan in order to make this book crisp yet effective.(mailing address has been provided at the end of the book on which you can mail with a subject of Sattvic diet plan to get the fundamental diet plan along with delicious and nutritious recipes which includes nutritious millet meals and detox beverages).

But this chapter is more than just a collection of recipes. It's a practical guide to mindful cooking and eating. Each recipe is an invitation to savor the process of preparing the food, to appreciate the colors, textures, and aromas, and to eat with awareness and gratitude. It's about making the act of eating a moment of mindfulness, a celebration of nourishment and life.

Important notes:

1.This body is just a heap of food, whatever you eat becomes a part of this body so it's not just a commodity it's life making material just like water. What type of food and how you eat it makes a complete difference how you experience life so eat with a sense of gratitude and reverence.

2.Before you start eating just sit and look at the food with gratitude. In that way this pause will make you conscious about how you should eat and how much you eat.

3.Before drinking water no Matter how thirsty you are just sit and hold the glass of water with both of your hands and look at it with gratitude and then drink it.This will change the molecular structure of water as water has memory and it will behave completely differently in your body.

4.First thing in the morning when you wake up drink 250ml of warm water(not hot water). Add honey, pinch of turmeric and pinch of powdered black pepper in it. Do not ingest anything for 30 min. This mixture will take care of any occult infection in the system and will maintain the gut health.(Alternative for coffee)

5.If you want to be super active then drink ash gourd juice empty stomach in the morning. It will cool your system and it's the most pranic(life energies)thing available on this planet.(add honey and black pepper if you have sinus and respiratory issues)

6.Always eat fruits empty stomach or 2 hrs before meal and should not be taken after meal as they take 2-2.5hrs to get digested and a meal(cooked food)takes 4-4.5hrs to get digested so the fruit will remain in your stomach for more than 2 hrs and all the nutrients will get destroyed. Best to eat for breakfast(you can add it in your Sattvic diet chart).

7.Include millets in the diet as they have 10 times more iron and calcium than wheat and rice. They reduce cholesterol and regulate blood pressure and blood glucose. They are gluten free so can be given to diabetic patients. They reduce the risk of colon(intestine)cancer significantly as they are rich in dietary fibre.(10 recipes have been provided which you can use it in the lunch)

8.Don't eat after 7:30PM as after sunset all of you biological processes will slow down including your digestive system and this will hamper your health and sleep. If you get late somehow then eat soft fruits like papaya.(No high water content fruits)

9.Use jaggery instead of sugar.(Not even artificial sweeteners)

10. Minimum 6hrs of gap between 2 meals because if you do snacking then body will involve only in digesting food and the excretion process at cellular level will hamper which will result in illness and cancer.

11. Fasting three times in a month will make you conscious about yourself by diverting your attention from the food, kill the cancer cells and regulate your sleep cycle.

12.Sit preferably on the floor in a cross legged posture while eating.(earth contact will make the food function in completely different way in your system)

Mindful Cooking Practices:

- Breath of Culinary Presence: Begin each cooking session with a few moments of conscious breathing, bringing your attention to the present moment and creating a calm and focused mindset.

- Ingredient Meditation: Before starting to prepare a dish, take a moment to connect with the ingredients. Appreciate their colors, textures, and aromas, and express gratitude for their nourishing qualities.

- Slow and Steady: Embrace a slower pace while cooking. Engage all your senses in the process, savoring the smells, sounds, and sensations that arise. Allow yourself to fully immerse in the culinary journey.

- Kitchen as Sanctuary: Create a tranquil atmosphere in your kitchen by decluttering the space, incorporating soothing scents, and playing soft music. Transform it into a sacred space where you can find peace and joy while cooking.

Fact: Studies have shown that cooking at home is associated with a healthier diet and a lower risk of obesity. It's a simple yet powerful way to take control of your health and wellness.

Mindful Eating Practices:

- Pause and Reflect: Before taking your first bite, pause for a moment of gratitude. Reflect on the effort and care that went into preparing the meal, as well as the nourishment it will provide your body.

- Engage Your Senses: As you eat, bring mindful awareness to each bite. Observe the colors, textures, and flavors. Chew slowly and savor the tastes. Notice the sensations and the way the food makes you feel.

- Mindful Portion Control: Tune in to your body's hunger and fullness signals. Eat until you feel satisfied, rather than eating out of habit or to finish everything on your plate. Pay attention to the signals of satiety and honor them.

- Digital Detox: Create a mindful eating environment by eliminating distractions such as smartphones, television, or other electronic devices. Focus solely on the food in front of you and the experience of eating.

- Mindful Mealtime Rituals: Gratitude Practice: Before starting your meal, express gratitude for the food, the hands that prepared it, and the nourishment it provides. Take a moment to appreciate the abundance and the interconnectedness of all beings involved in bringing the food to your plate.

- Silent Meal: Occasionally, have a silent meal where you

eat in complete silence. This practice allows you to deepen your connection with the food and your own sensations. Notice how it feels to eat without distractions and to focus solely on the act of eating.

- Mindful Conversation: Engage in meaningful and mindful conversation while sharing a meal with loved ones. Practice active listening, speaking from the heart, and creating a space of connection and presence.

- Mindful Eating Journal: Keep a journal where you record your thoughts, sensations, and reflections on your eating experiences. This practice can deepen your awareness of your relationship with food and help you identify patterns and preferences.(Everyday before sleeping just write one thing for which you are grateful today and sleep with that, life will change)

Embrace the invitation to immerse yourself fully in the art of mindful cooking and eating, allowing the flavors, textures, and aromas to ignite your senses and awaken a deeper appreciation for the nourishment that food brings to your life. Let this chapter be your guide on a delectable journey towards cultivating a deliciously conscious connection with every culinary creation and mindful feast.

In the next chapter, we'll delve deeper into mindfulness practices that you can incorporate into your everyday life, beyond the dining table. But for now, let's roll up our sleeves and embark on this culinary journey of Sattvic eating and mindful cooking.

6

Mindfulness Practices for Everyday Life

Section 1: Incorporating Mindfulness into Your Daily Routine

All the suffering is of mind and body so all these practices are aimed to make a distance between you and your body, you and your mind. This will result in lowering of your persona and you will make decisions not based on your likes and dislikes but on what the situation demands and that what is conscious living. let's explore.

Mindful Morning Rituals:

- Rise and Shine Mindfully: Begin your day by taking a few moments to stretch, breathe deeply, and set positive intentions for the day ahead.(Make a journal and write how your day should be like and what are your plans for today)

- Mindful Hygiene: Pay attention to the sensations and movements as you brush your teeth, wash your face, and take a shower. Feel the water on your skin and relish in the freshness of each moment.

- Mindful Eating: Mindful Breakfast: Treat yourself to a mindful breakfast experience. Take a moment to truly see, smell, and taste your food. Chew slowly and savor the flavors, allowing yourself to fully enjoy the nourishment it provides.

- Mindful Movement: Walking Meditation: Instead of rushing through your walks, slow down and embrace each step. Feel the ground beneath your feet, notice the rhythm of your breath, and take in the beauty of your surroundings.

- Mindful Exercise: Whether you're practicing yoga, going for a run, or doing any form of exercise, be fully present in each movement. Feel the stretch in your muscles, notice your breath, and appreciate the strength and vitality of your body.

Fact: Emerging research suggests that practicing mindfulness meditation can actually influence gene expression. Mindfulness has been found to downregulate genes associated with inflammation and stress response while upregulating genes associated with immune function and overall well-being.

Section 2: Mindfulness Exercises for Stress Relief and Improved Focus

- Breath Awareness: Calming Breath: Take a deep breath, allowing your belly to expand like a balloon. Slowly release the breath, feeling a sense of calm washing over you. Repeat this a few times whenever you need a moment of relaxation.

- Box Breathing: Imagine tracing the sides of a box with your breath. Inhale for a count of four, hold for four, exhale for four, and rest for four. This simple exercise can bring a sense of focus and tranquility.

- Mindful Pause: Three-Minute Breathing Space: Take three minutes to pause, breathe, and check in with yourself. Notice your thoughts, emotions, and sensations without judgment. Allow yourself to simply be in the present moment.

- Sensory Check-In: Engage your senses by tuning in to what's happening around you. Notice the colors, sounds, scents, tastes, and textures of your surroundings. This practice helps anchor you in the present and enhances your sensory experience.

Fact: Slow, intentional breathing activates the body's relaxation response and helps reduce the production of stress hormones such as cortisol,promoting a sense of calm and balance.

- Gratitude Practice: Gratitude Journal: Each day, write down something you are grateful for. They can be simple joys, moments of kindness, or things that bring you happiness. This practice helps shift your focus towards positivity and appreciation.(Gratitude pages have been provided in the end)

- Gratitude Meditation: Set aside a few minutes to reflect on the blessings in your life. Close your eyes, breathe deeply, and bring to mind the things you are grateful for. Allow yourself to feel a sense of warmth and appreciation in your heart.

Fact: Studies have shown that practicing gratitude can positively impact both mental and physical health. Gratitude exercises activate the brain's reward system, release feel-good neurotransmitters like dopamine and serotonin, and have been associated with reduced stress, increased resilience, and improved overall well-being.

Special meditation:

- Sit down daily comfortably on the ground with crossed or stretched out legs(right leg over left)with hands facing upwards over your thighs, close your eyes and watch your thoughts(don't create new thoughts and don't identify them as a good or bad as they are just thoughts)Your mind will take you somewhere from time to time and in between you will realize that oh!! I am sitting in meditation and watching my thoughts and that moment of realization is called thought awareness and with practice this window period(drowning into the thought to realize it's a thought)will decrease slowly and one day there will be a clear difference between you and your mind and that's the end of suffering my friend.
- Close your eyes and just imagine you have just one month to live and right from this moment what you wanna do. Visualize it intricately with small details and feel every sensation and emotions to its extreme while thinking what you want to do.Trust me your life will change and remember there's a 50/50 probability of you dying in the next moment so be aware always that you are mortal.

Remember that mindfulness is not a destination, but a continuous journey of self-discovery and growth. Embrace the opportunities to explore mindfulness in different aspects of your life, with curiosity and an open heart.

7

Conclusion: Your Journey Towards Wellness

Final Thoughts and Encouragement

As we conclude this remarkable journey, let us reflect on the transformative power of Sattvic eating and mindfulness. Throughout this book, we have uncovered the philosophy, science, and practical applications of these practices.

Now, it is time for your own journey towards health and wellness. Embrace Sattvic eating and mindfulness as lifelong companions, nurturing your body, mind, and spirit. Make mindful choices in your food, savoring each bite with gratitude and awareness.

But remember, this journey is not just about the food you eat. Extend mindfulness into every aspect of your life. Cultivate loving connections, find purpose in your work, prioritize self-care, and embrace personal growth with resilience.

Trust in your own strength and know that setbacks are part of the journey. Embrace self-compassion and patience as you navigate the path towards long-term health.

You are not alone on this journey. Seek support from loved ones, like-minded individuals, or professionals who can guide and inspire you. Surround yourself with a community that uplifts and supports your pursuit of health and wellness.

As you step forward into a future of vitality and well-being, carry the wisdom and practices shared in this book with you. Embrace each day as an opportunity to nourish your body, awaken your senses, and nurture your soul.

May your journey be filled with radiant health, joy, and inner peace. Embrace the power within you to transform your health and wellness.

Thank you for joining us on this transformative journey. Wishing you continued success and well-being.

Fact: Research has revealed that our breath not only influences our physical and mental well-being but also has the potential to affect the world around us. Studies on group meditation and intentional breathing practices have shown a phenomenon called the "Maharishi Effect." This effect suggests that when a critical mass of individuals engages in synchronized, positive intention through breath-focused practices, it can lead to reduced crime rates, increased social harmony, and even improved overall well-being in the surrounding community. This fascinating finding highlights the profound interconnectedness between our breath, our internal state, and the collective consciousness of humanity.

Your thoughts matter. If this book has touched your life, please take a moment to share your review. Your words have the power to inspire others on their journey towards mindfulness and wellness. Leave a review and be a part of the transformative ripple effect."

Note: consciousrevolution786@gmail.com (For fundamental diet, recipes and any other queries)

8

Ignition Through Your Words

"Dear reader, your journey through 'Mindfulness Guide for Beginners: The Sattvic Path to Wellness' is a testament to your commitment to self-discovery and inner growth. Your experience with this book is deeply cherished, and your insights hold immeasurable value. I humbly request that you share your heartfelt review, as your words have the power to ignite a spark of inspiration in someone else's life. Together, let us create a tapestry of transformative stories, woven with the threads of mindfulness, compassion, and well-being. Thank you for being a part of this extraordinary journey."

9

Fun Food Facts

- Honey never spoils. Archaeologists have found pots of honey in ancient Egyptian tombs that are over 3,000 years old and still perfectly edible.

- Carrots were originally purple. The familiar orange color of carrots that we know today was developed by Dutch growers in the 17th century, selectively breeding orange varieties.

- Apples float in water because they are made up of 25% air, giving them buoyancy.
- The world's most expensive spice is saffron. It takes around

150 flowers to produce just one gram of saffron, making it highly valuable.

- Cashews are not actually nuts, but rather seeds that grow on the bottom of cashew apples.

- Strawberries are the only fruit with their seeds on the outside. Each strawberry can have around 200 seeds.

- The world's largest pizza was made in 2012 in Italy and measured 131 feet in diameter.

- The durian fruit is known for its strong smell, often described as a mix of gym socks and rotten onions. It is banned in some hotels and public transport systems in Southeast Asia.

- Chocolate was once used as currency. The ancient Mayans and Aztecs valued cocoa beans so highly that they were used as a form of currency.

- The world's hottest chili pepper is the Carolina Reaper. It measures over 2 million Scoville Heat Units (SHU) and is known to cause intense heat and spice.

About the Author

Dear Reader,

As we come to the end of this book, I want to share with you a deeply personal journey that has shaped my path as a yoga practitioner and doctor. It is a journey born out of a profound empathy for the suffering I have witnessed, and a burning desire to transform the lives of those in need.

In the depths of my practice, I have encountered individuals burdened by the weight of their pain—physical, emotional, and spiritual. Their stories etched upon my heart, their struggles becoming my own. I have felt the desperate longing for healing, for a guiding light to lead them out of the darkness.

It is from this place of empathy that I embarked on a quest to not only ease their suffering but to empower them to rise above it. I delved into the depths of meditation, exploring the profound stillness and inner peace it could offer. I pursued my medical studies with unwavering determination, seeking knowledge and expertise to address the complex layers of human health and well-being.

Through years of practice, research, and witnessing countless miracles, I have come to understand that true transformation lies not only in the alleviation of symptoms but in the awakening of our inner power and potential. It is in embracing the practices of mindfulness, conscious living, and the nourishment of body and soul that we can truly heal and thrive.

Now, standing before you, I offer this book as a testament to the transformative power within each and every one of us. It is a roadmap, guiding you towards a life of wholeness and well-being. But it does not end here.

I invite you to join our revolutionary community, the heart of the Conscious Revolution. Within this sacred space, you will find solace, support, and a network of fellow seekers dedicated to their own personal growth and the upliftment of humanity.You will gain access to a treasure trove of resources, healthy delicious recipes, live events, and ongoing support. Imagine a space where there's no place for judgements, just like-minded individuals who will uplift and inspire you every step of the way.

By joining the Conscious Revolution community, you become an agent of change, carrying the torch of compassion and healing into the lives of others. Together, we can create a world where suffering is met with understanding, where transformation is ignited, and where the inherent potential within each individual is realized.

I implore you to embrace this opportunity, to join us on this profound journey of healing and transformation [https://chat. whatsapp.com/JwbyGUP6ylRI36w1VyLYbb
    to the Conscious Revolution community] and become a

cherished member of our revolutionary family. Together, let us transcend suffering and bring forth a world where true well-being flourishes.

With heartfelt compassion and unwavering dedication,
   Dr.Akhil

You can connect with me on:
🌐 https://chat.whatsapp.com/JwbyGUP6ylRI36w1VyLYbb

Printed in Great Britain
by Amazon